Spelling & Word-Power Skills - Book 1

Who is this book for?

This book is designed for three groups of students. The first group is the 5 to 7 year olds, who are working towards Key Stage 1 and SATs Assessment Tests. If you are in this group, then you are at the beginning of your Primary School stage.

The second group is made up of 7 to 12 year olds, who work independently at home or in school. All of the books in this series are free-standing, so a child can work through each of them or focus on the individual subject needs of the child.

The third group is made up of students who are preparing for 11+ exams for independent and grammar schools. This book provides a comprehensive course in spelling, and vocabulary development at this stage; together with comprehension and word-power development skills, needed for both verbal reasoning and creative writing.

Whichever group you belong to, your confidence and competence will grow, as you practice and improve your knowledge for life with these exercises. As your knowledge of English vocabulary expands, you will be excited and motivated by your developing skills and improved performance, not only in school but in life generally.

About This Book

This book **supports the whole of the Key Stage 1 and 2 English curriculum** for success in literacy. It will help you to develop your vocabulary and spelling skills so that you can be successful in learning English. You will not only learn new words and build your vocabulary (word bank) thoroughly, but you will also be motivated to extend your understanding and demonstrate this in both school work and out of school activities.

The books in this Series are:

- *English Grammar: A Student's Companion*
- *Mastering Comprehension Skills Books 1, 2 & 3*
- *11+ Preparation English Test Papers*
- *Vocabulary Skills for Students & Teachers Volumes 1 & 2*
- *Spelling &Word-Power Skills Books 1 & 2*

How the book is organized

This innovative approach to spelling development skills has been used by the author in classrooms for over 20 years, among children as young as 5 years. It was witnessed that deliberately teaching spelling as a subject and making linkages to the meaning of the words to situations they already knew, in an animated and fun way, made their experiences rich and alive with excitement. English became for those children, an exciting and fascinating subject that they excelled in, as they tried out their new-found word power in their written and spoken English. As a result, many succeeded in State Grammar school 11+ examinations and Independent school selection tests; as well as Year 6 pupils achieving and performing well above the expected levels in SATs.

Grading in the Book

The Spelling & Word Power Skills books cover 3 levels of practice, arranged from Starters (which introduces the structure of words, sounds and rules), **Level 1** (expands knowledge of phonics and increases the level of structuring of words and rules which guide them), **Level 2 and Level 3** (provides more challenges in exercises and rules that provides a structure within which the child is equipped with more advanced tools to learn, understand and spell at more advanced levels). Each level introduces spelling concepts, with explanation to help establish the rules which guide the approach to spelling techniques at each grade. Rules are identified and practice is given in exercises that test understanding. Practice exercises for you to complete, test your understanding of the rules applied. The fact is, we all have to spell words when we write. However, in English you will find there are lots of times when it's difficult to spell words for different reasons:

- The words are not spelt the way they sound
- They have an unusual combination of letters
- They don't follow the rules for the sounds you say
- Some have different rules that are no explainable
- The spelling of some words change according to how we use them.

These challenges can sometimes make spelling quite tricky. Why is this so? Well there have been many different influences from a wide background that have made English what it is today. The language is constantly being added to; therefore change is the only constant, as the language continues to evolve. In this book to help you spell correctly, there are spelling strategies that look at the certain aspects of the structure of words. Additionally some word hunt challenges help you to become aware of the make-up of words, forcing a closer look at word formation in full.

One of the first things to know is that words are made up of letters of the alphabet. The alphabet has 26 letters (21 consonants and 5 vowels). The **Vowels** are **a,e,i,o,u.** All other letters in the alphabet are called **Consonants.** Nearly all English words contain at least one vowel. Vowels can make a short or long sound. Therefore we begin our study in this book by firstly looking at the short and long vowel sounds, with exercises to help you avoid making common spelling mistakes.

A *Certificate of Achievement* is provided at the end of the book to give you a sense of reward for your hard work in completing the book. **Answers** are also provided at the back of the book to help you mark and evaluate your progress.

The right of Roselle Thompson to be identified as the author of this work has been asserted by her in accordance with the Copyright, Designs & Patents Act 1988.
All rights reserved. No part of this publication may be reproduced in any material form (including photocopying or storing it in any medium by electronic means and whether or not transiently or incidentally to some other sue of this publication), without the written permission of the copyright owner, except in accordance with the provisions of the Copyright, Designs and Patents Act 1988. Applications for the copyright owner's written permission to reproduce any part of this publication should be addressed to the publisher – *Eagle Publications.* British Library Cataloguing in Publication Data. A CIP record of this book is available from the British Library.

Warning: The doing of an unauthorized act in relation to this copyright work may result in court action as a claim for damages and criminal prosecution.

Published in the UK by: Eagle Publications, P O Box 73374, London W3 3FZ, UK
Email: eaglepublications58@gmail.com   www.eaglepublications.co.uk
Enquiries: 07739655603/07848844377

Cover Design: V3 Creative Designs

ISBN 978-0-9542325-5-9

© 2018 Roselle Thompson

Phoenix Study Guides

Spelling & Word-Power Skills

Book 1

By

Roselle Thompson

This book belongs to:

Name……………………………………………………………………………

EAGLE PUBLICATIONS

© 2018 Roselle Thompson   *Spelling & Word-Power Skills* Book 1

CONTENTS PAGE

STARTERS – *Short Vowel Sounds*   2
Short *a* Sound   2
Short *e* sound   8
Short *i* Sound   14
Short *o* sound   19
Short *u* sound   24

LEVEL 1 – *Long Vowel Sounds*   32
Long *a* sound   32
Long *e* sound   36
Long *i* sound   39
Long *o* sound   42
Long *u* sound   44
Words with *oo*   46
Practice Activity   47
Words with *oi* and *oy* blends   49
Words with *st* and *sl* blends   50
Words with *sh* blends   52
Words with *sp* blends   53
Words with *cr* and *dr* blends   55
Words with *br* and *gr* blends   57
Words with *ai* blends   59
Words with *i_e* form   61
High Frequency words for 7-8 year olds   63

Answers   66

Certificate of Achievement   68

About the Author & Other books in the Series   70

Phoenix Spelling Book

Phoenix Spelling & Word-Power Skills has been designed to help students learn and understand how words are structured in a graded approach to learning. It is organized so that each group of spelling can be learnt in a developmental way, since children learn at different speeds. Teachers and parents will be able to monitor children's learning, help reinforce and test their knowledge beginning with children in Reception classes of Primary Schools; up to the ages of 12 years old and beyond (Key Stages 2 & 3).

GRADED LEARNERS

This **Spelling and Word-power Skills** book covers **3 levels of practice**, arranged from **Starters** (which introduces the structure of words, sounds and rules), **Level 1** (expands knowledge of phonics and increases the level of structuring of words and rules which guide them), **Level 2 and Level 3** (provide more challenges in exercises and rules that present a structure within which the child is equipped with more advanced tools to learn, understand and spell at more advanced levels).

In addition to the words introduced at each of the 3 levels in this book, there is an extra list of **540 words**, aimed at those who have reached **Level 3 and beyond**.

The first thing you will notice about this book is the different ways of writing sounds. Although we say the letter sound, the writing of sound uses the International Phonetic Alphabet (IPA) and this is presented as follows:

a/ei/ sound	e/i/ sound	i/ai/ sound	o/eu/ sound	u/u:/ sound	u/ju:/sound
ai	ee	igh	oa	oo	ue
ay	e_e	ei	o	ue	ew
a_e	ey	i_e	o_e	u_e	u_e
a	ie	i	o_e	ew	you
ey	ei	ui	ow	o	u
ea	ea		eau	ou	
	i_e		ough	ough	
				ui	
				u	

You will still need to look out for different sounds from some familiar letter groups. For example, looking at the first box you will notice the 6 different ways of writing the letter **a**. However, there are other letter groups that make the **a** sound also e.g. *eigh* as in *...eight*; *ei* as in *...rein* and *ae* as in *...sundae*. In fact, you will encounter some exceptions to the rules and variations that make the whole experience of learning to spell quite interesting.

STARTERS

The *Short Vowel* sounds spelling contain 5 vowels: - **a e i o u**

In this book we practice each sound with at least 3 different letter endings, to reinforce knowledge of the sound. Once you know your alphabet sounds, (as well as all your capital letters), you will find that **Sound combination** (putting the letter sounds together), is a great way to begin to read.

Let's begin and remember to sound each letter sound separately, to hear the whole word sound, e.g. **c – a – t = cat**

Short (a) sound

a with (t) endings	a with (d) endings	a with (n) endings
c-a-t	d-a-d	c-a-n
s-a-t	m-a-d	p-a-n
r-a-t	p-a-d	r-a-n
f-a-t	h-a-d	f-a-n
b-a-t	s-a-d	m-a-n
h-a-t	b-a-d	b-a-n

© 2018 Roselle Thompson   *Spelling & Word-Power Skills* Book 1

WHAT YOU MUST DO NOW

Now put the letter *n* at the end to make a *short a* sounding word.

fa…   ca….   ra…   ma….   pa…

Now put the letter *t* at the end to make a *short a* sounding word.

sa…   pa…   ma….   ra…   fa…

Now put the letter *d* at the end to make a *short a* sounding word

ha…   da….   sa…   ba…   pa….

Now complete these mixed ending words with the *short a* vowel sound.

h…d   m….n   h….t   s…..t   d……d

f…..t   c….n   r….n   p….n   m….t

s……d   m….d   r….t   c….t   f…..n

© 2018 Roselle Thompson   *Spelling & Word-Power Skills* Book 1

On each line below there is a word that does not belong to the group. Underline the word.

Example: l**e**t p**e**t p**a**t m**e**t m**e**g

1. man   can   sad   pan   ran   fan
2. bat   sat   rat   mad   fat   hat
3. dad   sad   pad   cat   had   bad

Draw a line to match the words on one side with the same letter ending on the other side.

Now that you can say and write all the words with a sound, you need to learn three extra new words to help you to read.
Write these words several times and say them out aloud as you write them.

Your new words are …*here*…… *is*   and ….*the*

Now you have learnt the words...*here...is....the*, let's begin to put these words in a sentence. <u>Say</u> the words as you <u>write</u> the sentence.

1. Here is a cat. ....
2. Here is a mat. ....
3. Here is a rat. ....
4. Here is a bat. ....
5. Here is a hat. ....
6. Here is a fat cat. ....
7. The man is here. ....
8. The bad cat is here ....
9. A pan is here. ....
10. Here is a cat on a mat. ....

Now let's change the words around and begin to <u>read</u> with the letter *a*.

A cat is here..

A mat is here..

A rat is here..

A hat is here..

© 2018 Roselle Thompson   *Spelling & Word-Power Skills* Book 1

Let's read *short a* vowel words in a sentence. Read and write these sentences as often as you can.

1. Dad is here..
2. Here is a pan...
3. Here is a mat...
4. A fan is here...
5. A bat is here...
6. Here is a sad man..
7. A cat sat here...
8. The mad rat is here...
9. Here is dad..
10. The fat cat is here...

Reading *short a* with mixed techniques - different letter endings

1. Here is dad. Dad has a bat.

2. Here is Pat. Pat has a bag.

3. Here is a sad cat.

4. Sam is here. Sam has a bat.

5. Sam can bat.

6. Here is a man. The man has a car.

7. Here is Dan. Dan has a cat.

8. Dan can bat.

9. Pat can bat.

10. Here is Sam.

Tips for Short a/ei/ sound

There are other letter groups that make this sound also.

Examples are: *eigh* as in n*eigh*; *ei* as in r*ei*n and *ae* as in sund*ae*.

Now go onto the next sound!

Short (e) sound

e with (t) endings	e with (n) endings	e with (d) endings
m-e-t	p-e-n	b-e-d
g-e-t	m-e-n	t-e-d
l-e-t	t-e-n	r-e-d
s-e-t	h-e-n	e-n-d
b-e-t	b-e-n	l-e-d
w-e-t	d-e-n	w-e-d

WHAT YOU MUST DO NOW

Now put the letter *n* at the end to make a *short e* sounding word.

    pe…   te….   de…   me….   he…

Now put the letter *t* at the end to make a *short e* sounding word.

    se…   pe…   me….   ge…   we…

Now put the letter *d* at the end to make a *short e* sounding word.

    re…   be….   te…   le…   we….

© 2018 Roselle Thompson   *Spelling & Word-Power Skills* Book 1

Now complete these mixed ending words with the *short e* vowel sound.

b....d   m....n   g....t   s.....t   d....n

w.....t   l....t   m....t   p....n   b....t

t......n   d....n   r....d   p....t   h.....n

On each line there is a word that does not belong to the group. Underline the word.

Example: let p**e**t p**a**t m**e**t m**e**g

met	pet	set	pet	hen	get
bed	red	rat	led	wed	ted
pen	sad	hen	ten	men	ben

Draw a line to match the words on one side with the same letter ending on the other side.

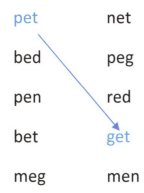

pet   net
bed   peg
pen   red
bet   get
meg   men

© 2018 Roselle Thompson   *Spelling & Word-Power Skills* Book 1

> **Now that you can say and write all the words with a sound, you need to learn three extra new words to help you to read. <u>Write</u> these words several times and <u>say</u> them out aloud as you write them.**

Your new words are …*here* ….. *is*   and ….*the*

> **Now that you have learnt the word…*here*…*is*….*the*, let's begin to put these words in a sentence. <u>Say</u> the words as you <u>write</u> the sentence.**

Here is a pen. ……………………………………………………………………

Here is a bed. ……………………………………………………………………

Here is a net.……………………………………………………………………

Here is Ben. ………………………………………………………………………

Here is a red hen. ………………………………………………………………

Here is a wet net. ………………………………………………………………

Now let's change the words around and begin to <u>read</u> with the e sound. <u>Write</u> the sentences.

A pen is here..

A net is here...

A bed is here..

A wet bed is here..

A pet is here...

The pen is here...

Meg has ten eggs...

Ted met Ben...

Sam has a red pen in the bag..

Let's read *short e* vowel words in a sentence. <u>Read</u> and <u>write</u> these sentences as often as you can.

1. Ben is here..

2. Here is a pen..

© 2018 Roselle Thompson   *Spelling & Word-Power Skills* Book 1

3. Here is a bed..
4. A bed is here..
5. A hen is here..
6. Here is a wet net..
7. A wet net is here..
8. The bed is here ....
9. The red pen is here ....
10. A pen is here. ....

Mixed techniques: *(Short e and some a sounds)* **with different letter endings –** *t, n, d, g.*

1. Here is Ben..
2. Ben has a net. ....
3. Here is Ted..
4. Ted has an egg..
5. Here is a wet bag. ....
6. Sam is here..
7. Ben is here..
8. Sam can bat..
9. Ben can bat..
10. Here is Meg..

11. Meg is a red hen……………………………………………………………………

12. Ted is here………………………………………………………………………

13. Ted has a red pen………………………………………………………………

14. The net is wet……………………………………………………………………

15. Pat has ten eggs…………………………………………………………………

16. The bed is in here………………………………………………………………

17. Pat wet Ben………………………………………………………………………

18. Here is a red pen…………………………………………………………………

Tips for Short e /i:/ sound

There are other letter groups that make this sound also. Examples are: *ie* as in the word bel*ie*ve and *ei* as in the word rec*ei*ve. The "i before e except after c" rule will help here. Another letter also makes this sound – it's the letter…. *y* as in happ*y*, mone*y*, carr*y*, bab*y*.

Now go onto the next sound!

Short (i) sound

i with (n) endings

i-n

b-i-n

t-i-n

p-i-n

s-i-n

i with (t) endings

i-t

h-i-t

s-i-t

l-i-t

b-i-t

i with (d) endings

h-i-d

d-i-d

l-i-d

k-i-d

b-i-d

WHAT YOU MUST DO NOW

Now put the letter *n* at the end to make a *short i* sounding word.

bi...   ti....   pi...   i....   si...

Now put the letter *t* at the end to make a *short i* sounding word.

si...   pi...   bi....   hi...   li...

Now put the letter *d* at the end to make a *short i* sounding word.

li...   hi....   di...   ki...   bi....

Now complete these mixed ending words with the *short i* vowel sound.

h...d   p....n   h....t   s.....t   d...d

f.....n   w....n   r....p   p....t   h....p

l......t   k....d   t....n   b....n   .....n

© 2018 Roselle Thompson   Spelling & Word-Power Skills Book 1

On each line there is a word that does not belong to the group. Underline the word.

Example: let   pet   p<u>a</u>t   met   meg

pin	can	sin	win	bin	tin
bit	sit	rip	mad	fit	hit
did	bid	pad	lid	hid	bid

Draw a line to match the words on one side with the same letter ending on the other side.

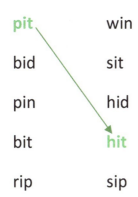

pit — win
bid — sit
pin — hid
bit → hit
rip — sip

Now that you can say and write all the words with a sound, you need to learn three extra new words to help you to read. Write these words several times and say them out aloud as you write them.

Your new words are …*here* ….. *is* and ….*the*

Now that you have learnt the words…*here* …*is*…. *the*, let's begin to put these words in a sentence. Say the words as you write the sentence.

Here is a tin. ....

Here is a pin. ....

Here is a bin. ....

Here is a pip. ....

Here is a lid. ....

Here is Tim. ....

Now let's change the words around and begin to read with the letter *i*

A bin is here..

A big lid is here..

A pin is here..

A tin is here..

A pit is here..

A big bin is here..

© 2018 Roselle Thompson　　　　　　　　　*Spelling & Word-Power Skills* Book 1

Let's read *short i* vowel words in a sentence. Read and write these sentences as often as you can.

1. A tin is here..
2. Here is a pin..
3. Here is a bin...
4. A fin is here..
5. A big pit is here...
6. Sit here...
7. Did Sid hit Tim?...
8. Here is Tim...
9. Here is a big bin..
10. Sid has a pin..

Mixed techniques *(short i and some a and e sounds)* with different letter endings: *t, n, d, g,*

1. Here is Ben..
2. Ben has a pin. ....
3. Here is Tim...

4. Tim has a pen………………………………………………………………

5. Here is a big bag. ………………………………………………………

6. Sam hit Ben…………………………………………………………………

7. Sit on the mat……………………………………………………………

8. Tim can bat…………………………………………………………………

9. Here is Meg………………………………………………………………

10. Meg has red lips………………………………………………………

11. Tim is here…………………………………………………………………

12. Tim has a big bed……………………………………………………

13. Get the red mat…………………………………………………………

14. Sam has a big red pen………………………………………………

15. I can sit on the bed…………………………………………………

16. The pen is in the bag………………………………………………

17. The cat bit the rat……………………………………………………

18. Tim is on his big red bed…………………………………………

Now go onto the next sound!

© 2018 Roselle Thompson

Short (o) sound

o with (t) ending	o with (p) ending	o with (g) ending
h-o-t	t-o-p	d-o-g
g-o-t	h-o-p	l-o-g
n-o-t	p-o-p	f-o-g
p-o-t	m-o-p	h-o-g
l-o-t		

WHAT YOU MUST DO NOW

Now put the letter *p* at the end to make a *short o* sounding word.

    po…   to….   mo…   ho….

Now put the letter *t* at the end to make a *short o* sounding word.

    no…   go…   lo….   po….   ho…

Now put the letter *g* at the end to make a *short o* sounding word.

    lo…   do….   ho…   fo…

© 2018 Roselle Thompson

Now complete these mixed ending words with the *short o* vowel sound.

h....t   m....p   h....g   l....g   n....t

d....g   t....p   p....p   p....t   h....p

g....t   f....g   d....t   c....t   l....t

On each line there is a word that does not belong to the group. Underline the word.

Example: let   pet   <u>pat</u>   met   meg

1. mop   pop   sit   top   hop   cop
2. got   rot   rat   pot   lot   hot
3. dog   log   pad   fog   hog   tog

Draw a line to match the words on one side with the same letter ending on the other side.

pot   lot

log   hop

top   tog

got   hot

hog   fog

© 2018 Roselle Thompson   *Spelling & Word-Power Skills* Book 1

Now that you can say and write all the words with a sound, you need to learn three extra new words to help you to read. Write these words several times and say them out aloud as you write them.

Your new words are ...*here* ..... *is*   and ....*the*

Now that you have learnt the word...*here*...*is*...*the*, let's begin to put these words in a sentence.   Say the words as you write the sentence.

Here is a log.   ....

Here is a dog.   ....

Here is a hot pot.   ....

Here is a mop.   ....

Now let's change the words around and begin to read with the letter *o*

A dog is here...

A log is here..

A pot is here..

A hot pot is here..

A mop is here..

© 2018 Roselle Thompson   *Spelling & Word-Power Skills* Book 1

Let's read *short o* words in a sentence. Read and write these sentences as often as you can.

1. A log is here………………………………………………………………………
2. Here is a pot………………………………………………………………………
3. Here is a mop……………………………………………………………………
4. A dog is here………………………………………………………………………
5. A hot pot is here…………………………………………………………………
6. Tom got a mop……………………………………………………………………

Mixed techniques *(short o and some a, e and i sounds)* with different letter endings: *t, n, d, g, p.*

1. Here is Tom…………………………………………………………………………
2. Tom has a mop……………………………………………………………………
3. Here is a dog. ……………………………………………………………………
4. Here is a hot pot. ………………………………………………………………
5. Tom is here…………………………………………………………………………
6. The dog is on the mat……………………………………………………………
7. Tom has a dog……………………………………………………………………
8. Here is Meg…………………………………………………………………………

9. Meg is on top of a box..

10. Tom is here..

11. Tom has a big box...

12. The boy is not here..

13. Sam has an egg..

14. Pat has a dog...

15. The dog is Lad...

16. The pot is hot..

17. A rat is on top of the box..

18. Ben can mop...

19. I can hop..

20. The boy is not here...

Now go onto the next sound!

Short (u) sound

u with (t) ending	u with (n) ending	u with (g) ending
b-u-t	s-u-n	h-u-g
c-u-t	r-u-n	m-u-g
h-u-t	g-u-n	r-u-g
n-u-t	b-u-n	d-u-g

WHAT YOU MUST DO NOW

Now put the letter *n* at the end to make a *short u* sounding word.

su…   ru….   gu…   bu….   fu…

Now put the letter *t* at the end to make a *short u* sounding word.

hu…   nu…   bu….   cu….   ru…

Now put the letter *g* at the end to make a *short u* sounding word

hu…   ru….   bu…   mu…   du…

Now complete these mixed ending words with the *short u* vowel sound.

h....t	m....g	h....g	r.....g	n....t
d....g	s....n	p....p	c....t	b....g
g.....	f....n	b....t	m....g	b.....n

On each line there is a word that does not belong to the group. Underline the word.

Example: let   pet   p<u>at</u>   met   meg

1. mug   cut   nut   hut   but   gut
2. hug   rot   rug   mug   bug   tug
3. sun   run   bud   gun   fun   bun

Draw a line to match the words on one side with the same letter ending on the other side.

pot   cut
hug   fun
sun   rug
gut   hot
bug   mug

(pot → hot shown as example)

© 2018 Roselle Thompson   Spelling & Word-Power Skills Book 1

Now that you can say and write all the words with a sound, you need to learn three extra new words to help you to read. <u>Write</u> these words several times and <u>say</u> them out aloud as you write them.

Your new words are ...*here* ..... *is*   and ....*the*

Now that you have learnt the word...*here*...*is*...*the*, let's begin to put these words in a sentence. <u>Say</u> the words as you <u>write</u> the sentence.

1. Here is a rug.   ....
2. Here is a mug.   ....
3. Here is a bug.   ....
4. Here is the sun.   ....

Now let's change the words around and begin to <u>read</u> with the letter *u*

1. A mug is here..
2. A rug is here..
3. A cup is here..
4. A nut is here..

© 2018 Roselle Thompson

Spelling & Word-Power Skills Book 1

Let's read *short u* words in a sentence. Read and write these sentences as often as you can

1. A rug is here...
2. Here is a nut..
3. Here is a cup...
4. A mug is here..
5. A hut is here...
6. The sun is hot...

Mixed techniques (*short u and some a, e, i and o sounds*) with different letter endings – *t, n, d, g, p.*

1. Tom has a nut..
2. Here is a big cup..
3. The pot is hot.... ....
4. Mum has a mug..
5. Lad the dog is on the rug. ....
6. Here is a hot mug. ....
7. Let us go now..
8. Ben can win...
9. We had fun in the sun...
10. Ben has a map for Sam..

© 2018 Roselle Thompson *Spelling & Word-Power Skills* Book 1

Mixed endings with short vowel sounds – a e i o u

(a) (e) (i) (o) (u)

(a)	(e)	(i)	(o)	(u)
pat	pet	win	hot	hug
had	ten	sit	got	nut
can	peg	hit	top	gun
cap	net	in	mop	sun
tap	let	pin	box	mug
bat	yes	dig	fog	rub
rat	yet	pig	fox	tub
fat	beg	six	dog	bud
jar	bed	his	now	mud
car	get	him	cow	fun
jam	bet	win	how	sum
day	den	tin	for	cup
bag	met	tip	pop	dug
map	wet	is	pot	run
sad	egg	it	not	rug

Choose from each list above, **write** ten of your favourite sound words in the boxes below.

	a	e	i	o	u
1.					
2.					
3.					
4					

© 2018 Roselle Thompson *Spelling & Word-Power Skills* Book 1

	a	e	i	o	u
4.					
6.					
7.					
8.					
9.					
10.					

Here are some more words for you to learn to help you to <u>read</u> and <u>write</u> by yourself.

are ……… look…… have……you……and

These are high frequency words, because they are used very often when we speak and write. <u>Learn</u> them, <u>write</u> them, and <u>use</u> them in your sentences.

Now <u>write</u> some sentences of your own using these words.

1. can……………………………………………………………………………………
2. peg……………………………………………………………………………………
3. hit………………………………………………………………………………………
4. top………………………………………………………………………………………
5. gun………………………………………………………………………………………
6. cap………………………………………………………………………………………

7. net..
8. in..
9. mop..
10. sun...
11. tap...
12. let..
13. pin...
14. box..
15. mug...

WHAT YOU MUST DO NOW:
READING

Try to <u>read</u> these sentences by yourself.

1. The boy can hop and the dog can run.
2. Look at Ben and his dog Lad.
3. The sun is hot and the boys are in the park.
4. Meg the red hen has ten eggs.
5. Can you cut the end of this bag?
6. I hug mum and mum hugs me.
7. Let's get a fan, it is hot in here.

© 2018 Roselle Thompson   Spelling & Word-Power Skills Book 1

8. The cat is on a rug in the sun.

9. I am wet but Sam is not wet.

10. Have you got a pet?

11. Mum has a big red car, it is here.

12. Mum put the hot pan in here.

13. The boy and his dad are not here.

14. Mr. Tom has six big fat pigs.

15. Can you look at Ben's map?

16. Look, I can do a sum.

17. I have six pins in my box.

18. Lad the dog likes to dig.

19. Let us go in mum's car now.

20. Tom and Ben are in bed.

Now score yourself and see how well you can read.

Score /20

If you can read more than **15** of these sentences, it means that you have done very well. If not, just keep practicing – practice makes perfect!

Well Done!! You *can* read!

Now go on to Level 1

© 2018 Roselle Thompson   *Spelling & Word-Power Skills* Book 1

Level 1

Long a sound – the different ways we can write it:

Sounds like the letter (a) (a_e/)		Sounds like the letter (a) (ay/ai/a/ey/ea)	
lake	bake	rain	snail
hate	fortunate	angel	holiday
date	plate	stay	delay
make	pale	wait	may
skate	sale	mail	laid
mistake	pane	prey	great
state	mane	play	maid
gate	manage	tail	train
safe	trace	paid	spray

1. Look at the different ways that *Long a* sound can be heard in these different types of word patterns:

    a_e = f*ate*; *ai* = tr*ai*n; *ay* = pr*ay*; *a*=*a*ngel; *ey*=pr*ey*; *ea*=gr*ea*t

2. Look at the words in the box above see if you can find these smaller words inside them. Circle them in the words above. For example - de<u>lay</u> = lay

    ate............   nail...............
    late............   it...................
    lay............   man...............
    take...........   stake.............
    fort............   age................
    ale.............   pan...............
    pray...........   mist..............
    day............   tuna..............

3. Look at the Long *a* words above. Now make 6 columns like the ones below and put the words above in their correct places.

ae	ay	a_i	ey	ea	a

Practice *Long a* sound – (a_e, ay, ai, ey, ea)- <u>Say</u> and <u>write</u> these

1. I may go to the shop today.

   ....

2. Can you say this word?

   ....

3. The dog has a long tail.

   ....

4. I paid for the milk.

   ....

5. This bed is on sale.

   ....

6. What is the date today?

   ....

7. I will make a cake.

   ....

8. He is at the gate.

   ....

9. What is his age?

   ....

10. It is going to rain.

    ....

11. Stay here for a while.

    ....

12. Get the mail from the post man.

    ....

13. Let us play in the rain.

    ....

14. I am going on holiday.

    ....

15. This is great.

    ....

16. I am going on a train today.

    ....

17. The maid is in the house.

    ....

18. I made a big mistake.

    ....

19. I am going to bake a cake today.

    ....

3. **Complete these sentences with words from this box.**

lake	bake	rain	snail
hate	fortunate	angel	holiday
date	plate	stay	delay
make	pale	wait	may
skate	sale	mail	laid
mistake	pane	prey	great
state	mane	play	maid
gate	manage	tail	train
safe	trace	paid	spray

1. They waited for the ....train............................to arrive at the station.
2. He put too much food on his…...….!
3. The dog is wagging its…………...……
4. What is today's ………………...…...?
5. Oops I made a ....in my work.
6. I can't ………………………...so I fell on the ice.
7. Will you ....….......................here until I get back?
8. We are going to Spain for our ………..……
9. Mum can ………………………..lovely cakes.
10. Tim and his friend broke a ………...................…..……of glass.
11. Sally …………………..for the sweets.
12. We have to wait at the ………….......................until someone opens it.
13. The groom brushed the horse's ………..
14. Wait till it's ....…........................to cross the road.
15. Our hen ....three eggs.

© 2018 Roselle Thompson   *Spelling & Word-Power Skills* Book 1

Long e sound

Here are groups of letters with Long e sound. Practise them often to learn the differences between them.

Sounds like the letter (e) (y/i/ea/ei/ie/i_e)		Sounds like the letter (e) (e/ee/e_e/ey)	
mummy	reason	me	these
happy	eat	deep	complete
taxi	reach	been	secret
heat	give	need	extreme
mean	read	keep	money
tummy	meat	feed	alley
silly	peaches	wheels	valley
treat	reach	be	turkey
bully	beat	teeth	kidney
teach	bleach	tree	greet
seat	funny	seem	donkey

Look at the many ways that Long e sound can be heard in these different types of word patterns:

>   y ending – *happy, silly*   e ending – *me, be*
>   i ending - *taxi,*   ee word pattern – *free, meet*
>   ea pattern – *read, teach,*   e_e word pattern – *these, extreme*
>   ie pattern – *field*   ei pattern – *receive*
>   i_e pattern - *marine*
>   *ey ending – e.g. *money, kidney*

* can be tricky as some *ey* ending have a long a sound. For example, *convey, survey*

WHAT YOU MUST DO NOW

1. Look at the *Long e* sound words above. Now make 10 columns like the one below and put the words above in their correct places.

y	e	i	ee	ea	e_e	ei	i_e	ie	ey

2. Find words in the box above which mean the *opposite* of these words

   sad…………………..   learn………………..…

   public……………….   hungry………………..

   serious……………..   mountain…..……..........

   part…………………   receive…………....……

   shallow……………..   generous……………...

3. **Complete these sentences with words from the box above.**

   1. I can …………………..............……….these sentences on my own.
   2. If I tell you a ………….........…………….. you should not tell anyone.
   3. Dad gave me some …………………...................................to buy sweets.
   4. My family had ………………..............................for dinner at Christmas.

5. The water in this pool is not very ……………………………………………..

6. Dan asked me to ……………………........................his goldfish for him.

7. My neighbour took a ……………...............................to the airport.

8. What is the ……………….......................……….for not doing your work?

9. Dogs eat lots of …………….................... and need lots of walk each day.

10. I brush my …………………..............................….two times each day.

11. My cat likes to climb an apple ….............................in our garden.

12. There is ....……..................in our car as the sun is very hot today.

13. For our picnic, we packed apples …...............…………….pears and plums.

14. "The ……………...............on the bus go round and round," sang the child.

15. Mum cleans our kitchen floor with ....……………

Now score yourself and see how well you did.

Score / 15

If you scored 15 well done!

Here is a ☆ for you.

Tip for Writing:

Remember your <u>Sentences</u> must <u>begin with a capital letter</u>

and <u>end with a full stop</u>.

© 2018 Roselle Thompson   *Spelling & Word-Power Skills* Book 1

Long i sound – the different ways we can write it:

Sounds like the letter (i) (i_e/y)		Sounds like the letter (i) (ie/i followed by gh)		(ie at the end of a word) and ui
side	supply	light	tight	died
bike	magnify	right	tonight	lie
slide	try	sight	fright	pie
drive	fly	might	flight	cried
hide	fry	fight	delight	spied
wide	reply	bright	night	disguise
pipe	satisfy	high	slight	fried
wine	deny	thigh	sigh	supplier
pile	cry	knight	height	tried

i_e = ride   y = cry   igh = fight   ie = lie   ui = disguise

WHAT YOU MUST DO NOW

1. Learn these Long *i* words. Copy them out in your exercise book and put them in the right sound box below. Say them aloud as you do write them.

ie	y	ei	igh	ui

2. **Choose the correct *Long i* sound from the boxes above and put them in their correct place in the words with gaps below.**

t........t   sl....d.....

fr.......t   del......t

repl......   m.........t

kn.......t   w......n...

suppl......   r........ ..t

n.........t   sp........d

ton.......t   fr........d

magnify.....   th.........

dr.....v.......   cr.......d

3. **Find words in the box above which mean the opposite of these words:**

day...........................   dark........................

loose........................   low........................

narrow.....................   truth......................

seek..........................   left.........................

laugh........................   born........................

4. **Complete these sentences with words from the box above.**

   1. Dad......................our blue car.

   2. Tom ....to do his best in his test.

   3. We play ....and seek in our garden.

   4. Dad ....6 eggs for our breakfast.

   5. "Go to the end of this room and turn................," he said.

6. She had a cut on her .... when she fell off the bed.
7. There is a ....light light in my room.
8. We are going to my aunt's house ....
9. He said that he likes meat..................................and chips.
10. I will ....this picture so that you can see it clearly.
11. Babies often ....when they are wet.
12. "I need a ....to my letter," said mum.
13. Tom's shoes are too ....he needs a bigger pair.
14. "You are very tall, what is your ....?" she asked.
15. It was a ....to watch this funny film with my friends.

Now score yourself and see how well you did.

Score /15

If you Scored 15 well done!

Here is a ⭐ for you!

Tips for adding ...*ing* to words ending in *ie*

When a word ends in ..*ie*, we need to change the ...*ie* to ...*y* before adding ...*ing*

Examples are as follows: l*ie* = l*y*ing; d*ie* = d*y*ing; t*ie* = t*y*ing

© 2018 Roselle Thompson

Long o sound – the different ways we can write it:

Sounds like the letter (o) (o_e/ow)		Sounds like the letter (o) (oe/o/oa) & eau/ough	
slope	show	gold	boat
snow	own	although	float
rope	cope	old	throat
throw	blow	toe	moat
note	grow	told	so
woke	row	foe	doe
hole	elbow	gateau	roast
drove	follow	no	goat
hope	stone	coat	dough

o_e = rope   ow = grow   oe = toe   o = no   oa = boat
eau = plateau   ough = although

WHAT YOU MUST DO NOW

1. Learn these different *Long o* sound words – copy the words and say them out aloud as you do so.

2. Choose the correct *Long o* sound from the boxes above and put them in their correct place in the gaps below.

dr....v.   r......st
h...p....   st...n...
thr....t   foll......
c.......t   gat......
m......t   elb......
thr.....   ....ld
fl.....t   w....k..
b......t   gr........
sl...p...   t..........
bl.......   g......ld

© 2018 Roselle Thompson

3. Find words in the box above which mean the *opposite* of these words:

young..................... let go............................

sink....................... buck...........................

friend..................... yes..............................

lead........................ hide............................

4. Complete these sentences with words from the sound box above.
1. The farmer has a ....and several sheep on his farm.
2. Let's ....bubbles in the garden.
3. You must all ....Tom as you go into the room.
4. I put my ....on a peg at the back of the class.
5. Ben fell and hurt his ....
6. A noise ....me up when I was sleeping.
7. Pete has his..pen, so he doesn't need yours.
8. Mum wrote a ....for my teacher.
9. Don't ....your ball in the garden next door.
10. Some of my toys can ....in water.
11. When the snow stops we will make a ....man in our garden.
12. I dug a ....in the play-ground during our lunch break.
13. ....we ran for the train, we still missed it.
14. The farmer has more than one ....on his farm.
15. We all like playing in the ....and making snowmen.

Now score yourself and see how well you did.

If you scored 15 well done! | /15

Here is a for you!

Long u sound – the different ways we can write it:

Sounds like the letter (u) (u_e)	Sounds like the letter (u) (oo/ou/o/ough/ui/u)			(ew or ue at the end of a word)	
route	group	Look	spoon	glue	screw
refuse	soup	good	room	due	view
consume	troupe	brook	stool	true	knew
cube	through	tooth	wool	blue	few
rule	coupon	root	truth	queue	drew
puke	youth	bloom	stood	chew	nephew
acute	should	spoon	shook	blew	review
tube	would	loop	fruit	grew	argue
rude	you	through	food	brew	new

u_e = r*u*l*e*   oo = t*oo*th   ou=s*ou*p   ough=thr*ough*

ui=br*ui*se   u=tr*u*th   ui=fr*ui*t   ew=dr*ew*   ue=tr*ue*

Tips: There are a few words which end in *ough* which do not have the same sound. **Examples are**: th*ough*, thr*ough*, d*ough*, bor*ough*, c*ough*, and th*ough*t.

There are some *ough* words which have the *f* sound in words like *cough*, *enough*, *tough*, *rough*

MORE Tips for writing the Long *u* Sound:
Here are some tips to help you spell Long *u* words:
   Tip 1. *oo*, *ou* and sometimes *ui* comes in the middle of a word
       e.g. c*oo*k, s*ou*p, br*ui*se
   Tip 2. *ew* or *ue* comes at the end of a word. e.g. tiss*ue*, thr*ew*
   Tip 3. *u_e* pattern – the *e* is silent e.g. r*u*d*e*, t*u*n*e*

WHAT YOU MUST DO NOW

1. **Learn these different *Long u* sound words – copy the words and say them out aloud as you do so.**

2. **Choose the correct *Long u* sound from the boxes above and put them in their correct place in the gaps below.**

   1. The tree has lots of leaves and …………..which grow underground.
   2. I know I ……………….........................……do my work quickly.
   3. The soldier ……………....................……..on guard outside the palace.
   4. We took the underground…........………….to go to Central London.
   5. The ………….................……fairy came when I lost my front tooth!
   6. I need a ……........................……..to eat my yoghurt.
   7. Let's look ………………..……….the window to see the rain falling.
   8. Dad will…………....................to let me go to my friend's sleep-over.
   9. "That story is ……..….,"said the little girl, "It happened yesterday."
   10. Mum took the …………............. for £1 discount to the supermarket.
   11. My mum's ……………….............…..is coming to visit us on Sunday.
   12. I like drinking hot ………….......................…….during the winter.
   13. The …….........................…….boy was sent to the Head teacher.
   14. I want some glitter and ………..........................……..for my picture.
   15. We all need to …………...........……..our food before we swallow it.

Now score yourself and see how well you did.

Score 15

If you scored 15 Well done!

Activity with OO Words

book	good	roof	loop
took	boot	root	shook
hood	cook	noon	spoon
pool	moon	rook	brook
cool	hook	broom	mood
soon	food	stood	stool
too	wood	tooth	wool
tool	foot	bloom	stoop
look	hoot	fool	moo

WHAT YOU MUST DO NOW

Complete these sentences with words from the box above.

1. I will read to you from my new..
2. We will ....for the lost pound coin.
3. My class is going to the swimming ....after lunch.
4. I sweep the garden with a ....
5. I have a wobbly ....
6. Mum cooks very delicious ....
7. Stay here I will be back..
8. There is a ....in the sky at night.
9. Dad is happy, he is in a good ....
10. My coat has a ....
11. You work is always very ....the teacher said.
12. Put your coat on the ....
13. We will have our lunch at ....
14. Men are working on the ....of our house.

Practice Activity

Now put these words in the correct sound list below.

cheese	hood	heel	soon	teeth
	defeat		bean	
deep		feed		steel
	reach		ate	
page		came		pay
	late		rake	
ray		age		grade
	snail		rail	
tool		book		name
	hoot		took	
geese		seen		mean
	toast		sore	
soak		coal		flow
	groan		loaf	
woke		trail		lean
	coach		cloak	
flow		roam		home
	slow		so	
float		vote		moan
	stone		cage	
keep		we		free
	stray		save	
plate		save		pain
	play		stay	
cool		soup		school
	group		bruise	
safe		name		stay
	delay		lace	
ride		grade		time
	shame		side	
chew		wine		slide
	grew		group	
cruise	pool	shade		argue
stool		suit	stew	few

Sounds like the letter (a) (a_e)		**Sounds like the letter (a)** (ai/ay)	

Sounds like the letter (e) (y/i/ea)		Sounds like the letter (e) (e/ee/e_e/ey)

Sounds like the letter (i) (i_e/y)		Sounds like the letter (i) (ie/i followed by gh)		(ie at the end of a word)

Sounds like the letter (o) (o_e/ow)		Sounds like the letter (o) (oe/o/oa)	

Sounds like the letter (u) (u_e)	Sounds like the letter (u) (oo/ou)			(ew or ue at the end of a word)	

Words with *oi* and *oy* in them

Words with *oi*		Words with *oy*	
oil	boil	joy	destroy
voice	coil	enjoy	boy
rejoice	poison	employ	annoy
coil	soil	buoy	ploy
ointment	choir	decoy	toy
foil	spoil		
coin	moist		
noise	join		

WHAT YOU MUST DO NOW

1. **Learn these *oi* and *oy* sound words by copying the words and saying them out aloud as you do so.**

2. **Look at the words in the boxes above. See how many of these smaller words you can find inside some of the *oi/oy* words above.**

| oil | son | in | joy | is | to | ice | an | troy | ploy |

3. **Complete the sentences with words from the word-list above.**

1. I can ……………………………………………………………an egg.
2. Tom gave him a new……………………………………for his birthday present.
3. He is not a girl, he is a ……………………………………………………………
4. There is too much………………………………………………………………in here!
5. I can give you a new pound ………………………………… for your piggy-bank.
6. I did ……………………………………………………………myself at your party.
7. Luke wants to ……………………………………………………………our game.
8. Ann has a loud……………………………………………………………………
9. My skin is ………………………………………………………from sweating a lot.
10. Mum put some ………………………………………………………on my bee sting.

Now score yourself and see how well you did.

If you scored 15, Well Done!   Here is a ⭐ for you!   /10

© 2018 Roselle Thompson   *Spelling & Word-Power Skills* Book 1

Words with *st* and *sl* blends

best	frost	slope	slum
rest	just	slam	sleet
rust	must	slap	slack
mist	sling	slim	slot
twist	east	slide	slab
west	cost	slip	slit
stem	dust	slime	slug
nest	strong	slow	slurp
blast	master	sleep	slight
past	star	slate	slave
fist	list	slap	stamp

WHAT YOU MUST DO NOW

1. **Make a list of 10 *st* and *sl* words from the box above and <u>underline</u> the *st* and *sl* blends.**

st words	*sl* words

© 2018 Roselle Thompson

2. **Look at the words in the *st/sl* box above. See how many of these smaller words you can find inside some of the words above.**

last	tar	low	lime	light	late	is	
as	mast	slim	ate	me	lap	lip	
slid	lack	lot	lab	lit	us		

3. **Complete the following sentences by putting the correct word from *st/sl* in the box above.**

   1. She walks as ……………..as a ……………….........................……
   2. Please don't …………………………………………………........the door!
   3. Here is a bird's ……………………………………………………..
   4. Mum put a ……………….......on the letter then she put it in the post box.
   5. I don't want to go to ………………………………..…. I am not tired.
   6. You………………………….....wash your hands before you eat.
   7. Let's ……………………………………………........down this slope.
   8. You are ………………….............……in time for the beginning of the play.
   9. The sun rises in the east and sets in the …………..........……..………
   10. We walk …………...............……….....……the sweet shops every day.
   11. It's not polite to ………….................…………….…………. your tea.
   12. You must …………………..the top to open the bottle.
   13. Tyrone hit David with his……………..………………………………….……
   14. The sun rises in the ....…........................and sets in the west.
   15. My teacher gave me a gold............................for doing good work.
   16. This lady is quite ....she is not fat.
   17. It's so cold there is ……………….............……………..on the window.
   18. We put our ten pence pieces in the …………..machine to play in the fair.
   19. My brother found a bird's………....…..on our apple tree in the garden.
   20. The cold weather caused ……………....…..and snow throughout the day.

Words with *sh*

shop	show	bush	ship
rash	shell	wash	rush
sheet	wish	brush	shine
dish	crush	should	fish
shell	shake	rush	push
shade	sheep	fresh	shame
shut	push	gush	shape
sharp	shelf	bush	shook
shadow	flesh	flash	finish

WHAT YOU MUST DO NOW

1. Look at the words in this box. See if you can find these smaller words inside some of the words above and circle them.

> ash   hook   harp   hell   ash   how   elf   ape   rush
> had   hut   she   hop   was   is   he   hip   in   is   us   bus

2. Complete these sentences with words from the box above.

   1. The farmer let us feed his ……………………………………………
   2. I am going to buy something from the ……………………………………
   3. You must ……………………………………your hands now.
   4. When I stand in the sun, it casts a ………………… behind me.
   5. The knife is ……………so you must be careful when you use it.
   6. You …………say sorry to your brother because you upset him.
   7. Can you ……………………………………me your lovely picture?
   8. I like ……………………………………and chips.
   9. I have many books on a ………………………… in my room.

Now score yourself and see how well you did.

If you scored 9   Well done!

Here is a ☆ for you.

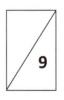

© 2018 Roselle Thompson

Words with sp

spot	spit	wasp	spent
spin	spend	spool	spike
spit	spoil	speak	spear
spread	spuds	spill	spur
sports	spoon	speed	spider
spin	respond	spade	spine
spade	clasp	spend	spell
wasp	spare	respect	inspect
hospital	sponge	response	special
suspense	spy	suspect	spread

WHAT YOU MUST DO NOW

You will notice that **sp** blends can be at the beginning, in the middle or at the end of a word. For example:

     ho**sp**ital   **sp**ecial   cla**sp**

1. Put a circle around the **sp** blend in the words in the box above.

2. Look again at the words in this box. See if you can find these smaller words inside some of the words above and circle them.

pool	end	read	ear	oil	port	read	pill
pin	pot	end	pear	pine	peak	was	
are	pens	in	pike	as	it	pit	

3. Complete these sentences with **sp** words from the box above.

1. Tom saw a ………………… in the bathroom but he is not afraid of it.
2. I am going to ………………… five pounds on books and sweets.

3. This is a ………………........... prize for doing very good work in school.

4. Anthony likes ………………….............. and his favourite is football.

5. Sally did not..………………….......the milk on the table, it was Ben.

6. My teacher said that she would like to ……......………..to me after class.

7. I often ………………................... butter on my bread at breakfast time.

8. My sister helps me ……….........................……..some words for my story.

9. Last summer I got stung by a ……..…………..

10. We went to the ....…............to see my aunt's new baby.

11. Have you got a …………….................................pen I could borrow?

12. He was driving at a fast..................….......................... when he crashed.

13. Another name for potatoes is ……………….............................…….........……

14. A long time ago men fought with ....…............. today they use guns.

15. In most movies, the ……………….......................... gets caught in the end.

16. The police stopped a man they said that was a ………......……….of a crime.

17. Jem used a ……………………..........to wipe spilt mild on top of the table.

18. The little boy ……………........his hands, closed his eyes, then said a prayer.

19. It is not good for anyone to ……...………….on the ground, it's unhygienic.

20. The audience waited in …………………. to see who the mystery guest was.

Now score yourself and see how well you did.

Score ⟋ 20

If you scored 20. That's Excellent!

Here is a ☆ for you.   Well Done!

Words with cr		Words with dr	
crush	crash	drop	drip
crown	crunch	drag	dream
cry	cream	drug	drum
crisp	creepy	drab	drench
cross	crowd	drink	drill
crab	crime	drought	driver
crate	cram	dress	dribble
crib	crack	drape	drift
cradle	crumb	dreary	driveway

WHAT YOU MUST DO NOW

1. Put a circle around the *dr and cr* blends in the words in the box above.

2. Look again at the words in this box. See if you can find these smaller words inside some of the words above and circle them.

ream	rush	rip	rate	rack	own	rush	rag
river	rug	rink	ought	ram		rear	way
rift	rum	run	row	creep	ate	rib	as	in
if	drive	rim	creep	ape	ear	way	ill

3. Complete these sentences with *cr* and *dr* words from the box above.

 1. I would like a …………………..........................of water please.

 2. There was a huge …………………..........................of people at the fair.

 3. The Queen wears a …………………..............................on her head.

4. I have a packet of cheese and onion ……………………………………………..
5. Mum bought me a new ……………….......................…………for my birthday.
6. Peter says that he hates ……………….…………………………….crawlies.
7. Mum told me not to ………………...…………………..my bag on the ground.
8. The men are going to ………………...……………………………….for oil.
9. Simon and I got ………………........................…………….in the heavy rain.
10. We put some sun block ……………..........................……….on our bodies.
11. The ……………….............................shouted when they saw the pop star.
12. My phone fell, now there is a ……………….…………….…in my screen.
13. The nursery children sang songs as I beat a...........................for them.
14. Reece is very good at football, he ……………….....................the ball very well.
15. We always park our car on our ………………….........…………………..

Now score yourself and see how well you did.

If you scored 15, Well Done!

/15

Here is a for you!

More spelling Tips: **Changing words from <u>singular</u> to <u>plural</u> form**	
Some words have no singular form and are always in the plural.	
deer	deer
salmon	salmon
sheep	sheep
cod	cod
Words ending in o or a vowel and o, add es to make them plural.	
cargo	cargoes
hero	heroes
potato	potatoes
tomato	tomatoes
volcano	volcanoes
Some words change completely when we make them plural	
policeman	policemen
child	children
tooth	teeth
goose	geese
ox	oxen

© 2018 Roselle Thompson   *Spelling & Word-Power Skills* Book 1

Words with *br*		Words with *gr*	
brown	brave	gravy	green
brake	bright	growl	grip
break	brisk	grasp	grapes
brim	bring	grand	great
broken	bride	grub	greet
breathe	bruise	grab	grill
brother	brush	grief	group
briefcase	brigade	grease	grandchild
brilliant	breeze	graceful	governor

WHAT YOU MUST DO NOW

1. **Put a circle around the *br and gr* blends in the words in the box above.**

2. **Look again at the words in this box. See if you can find these smaller words inside some of the words above and circle them.**

owl	grand	ease	race	rush	ride	ring	risk	
right	rave	other	case	eat	the	own	rake	
rim	child	broke	row	rid	rub	rake		
ill	and	rip	owl	row	rave	ant	grow	

3. **Find a word from the box** that is the *opposite* of the following:

   sister…………………   coward…………………

   groom…………………   mend…………………

   small…………………   happiness…………………

   drab…………………   dark…………………

4. Complete these sentences with *br* and *gr* words from the box above.

1   I fell and got a ……………………………………on my leg.
2   I like ………….............................with my meat and vegetables.
3   Dad put all his papers in his …………………......……before going to work.
4   Let's go for a …………….....................................walk around the park.
5   My Grandmother has one …………….....................………..and that's me!
6   After a hot day, there was a cool ……………......................………at night.
7   Mum pressed the ……………………………………………….to stop the car.
8   Our dog likes to ………………………………………………………..at strangers.
9   Our neighbour was full of …………….......................…..when her dog died.
10 The called the fire……………………………………………….to put out the fire.
11 The ballerina danced very ………………………………………………..on stage.
12 Fish can ………………………………………………………………..under water.
13 I …………….....................the railings tightly as we ran down the escalator.
14 A new …………….......................................has joined our school this term.
15 We had a …………….......................... after 60 minutes of hard work.

Now score yourself and see how well you did.   ⎡⎯⎯⎯⎤
                                                      ⎢ /15⎥
                                                      ⎣⎯⎯⎯⎦

If you scored 15, Well Done!

Here is a ☆ for you!

Tips for words ending in *f* or *fe*

When a word ends in …*f* or …*fe*, to make it plural, we leave out the …*f* or …*fe* and add …*ves*.

E.g. wi*fe*=wi*ves* - scar*f*=scar*ves* - loa*f*=loa*ves* - kni*fe*=kni*ves*

Words with *ai*

nail	hail	pain	sail
rail	rain	tail	fail
hail	pail	main	grain
faint	paint	wait	praise
remain	railway	frail	drain
trail	gain	wait	bait
mail	wail	bail	afraid
paint	maid	bait	raid
paid	train	refrain	drain

WHAT YOU MUST DO NOW

Put a circle around the *ai* blends in the words in the box above.

1. **Look again at the words in this box. See if you can find these smaller words inside some of the words above and circle them.**

main	aid	rain	way	in	raise	raid	rail	aid	it

2. **Complete these sentences with *ai* words from the box above.**

   1. We entered the building through the ....gates.
   2. Some children are ....of the dark.
   3. We ....£5.00 for our football socks.
   4. He is studying hard so he won't ....his test.
   5. You must.....................................here while I get our tickets.
   6. Please ....from shouting in class.
   7. Jack and Jill went up the hill with a ....to get water.

8. Dad is going to ....my room in my favourite colour.

9. The Head teacher will ....her for getting 100% attendance.

10. The fishermen tried to ....the fish with worms.

11. The boy said that he had a ....in his tummy.

12. In an hour's time the ship will ....away from the harbour.

13. The farmer harvested his ....at the end of the summer.

14. My dog wags its ....when it's happy.

15. The old woman is quite..............so she walks with a stick.

Now score yourself and see how well you did.

If you scored 15, Well Done!

/15

Here is a for you!

Tips for unusual plural formation

Some words have unusual plurals because they copy the plural forms from other world languages where they originate from: e.g. French, and Latin.

Singular	Plural	Singular	Plural
man	men	child	children
mouse	mice	sheep	sheep
deer	deer	oasis	oases
person	people	fungus	fungi
fish	fish	penny	pence or (pennies)

Some words which end in ...*f* and ...*o* may have two different ways of writing their plurals: Notice the different endings – *s, ves, es*

Examples are as follows:

carg*o* = either cargo*es* or cargo*s*

hoo*f* = either hoov*es* or hoof*s*

Words with *i_e*

hide	like	pipe	time
mine	line	wide	bike
strike	spine	grime	wide
nine	life	side	slide
drive	quite	fire	shine
vine	wide	slide	stripe
limes	live	wine	ride
dine	spite	hide	tile
hive	pride	beside	tide
mike	bite	wife	life
wipe	ripe	bite	knife
bike	mike	ripe	rise

WHAT YOU MUST DO NOW

1. **Put a circle around the *i_e* form in the words in the box above.**

2. **Look again at the words in this box. See if you can find these smaller words inside some of the words above and circle them.**

lid	ripe	side	if	pit	rid	rip
live	strip	slid	pin	ride	spin	vine
slid	trip	slim	it	rip	be	me
win	hid	fir	spit	in	pine	mine

3. **Complete these sentences with *i_e* words from the box above.**

   1. George wants to play ……………………………and seek with us.
   2. That ball is ……………………………………but you can play with it.
   3. The sun will ……………………………today, and it's going to be very hot.
   4. We ……………………………in the city so we take the underground.
   5. Our garden has grapes which grow on long ……………………………

6. Bees live in a ....where they make honey.
7. I......................going to the park with my friends.
8. We made a ....in the fireplace because it was quite cold.
9. I got a new ....for my birthday, and I can ride it.
10. The children took turns on the ....
11. The ....in our kitchen is white and blue in our bathroom.
12. Some people have ....with their meal.
13. I need to ....the wet floor.
14. Our school begins at ....o'clock.
15. The men are cleaning the dirt and ....from the drains.
16. He took a ....from his apple then threw it away.
17. Mum said that it was ....to go to bed.
18. We sat ....the camp fire and sang songs.
19. Sally takes ....in doing her work, that's why it's very neat.
20. We bought some lemons and ....in the supermarket to make juice.

Now score yourself and see how well you did.

Score 20

If you scored 20, that's Excellent!

Tips for words ending in *o* and *f*

When a word ends in an *o*, to make it plural, we just add *es*.
  E.g. potat*o* = potato*es*   tomat*o* = tomato*es*

However, you will still need to look out for some words ending in *o* and *f,* which need an *s* - not *es*! Examples are: **radio** = radio*s,* **piano** = piano*s*, **roof** = roof*s*

High Frequency Words for 7/8 year olds (380 words)

that	here	put	hair	add
there	when	help	more	after
their	where	play	house	fairy
they	out	help	more	sorry
then	what	open	near	sorry
this	put	made	hear	love
them	our	much	face	come
she	try	made	year	funny
her	have	nice	lady	coming
you	very	into	lady	making
your	said	little	speak	count
with	were	near	fire	find
some	said	eyes	happy	father
want	nice	talk	first	doing
are	every	walk	sick	mother
saw	ever	story	home	brother
sister	by	never	baby	other
by	ever	baby	give	dinner
try	down	water	butter	supper
kind	again	water	table	going
new	itself	just	goes	work
does	next	some	please	could
would	tried	next	later	upon
once	please	anything	tea	door
drive	just	clock	only	girl
round	ground	found	thing	small
about	same	over	more	week
name	night	turn	dance	great
next	later	cousin	name	night
turn	next	later	cousin	whole
early	time	number	behind	nothing
key	use	better	many	try

why	who	hour	ask	which
speak	walk	talk	think	become
open	tomorrow	baby	tiny	where
upon	once	young	fairy	story
live	last	happily	after	upon
number	right	three	friend	moment
money	done	bright	stand	pretend
long	fight	pretty	person	close
join	start	five	easy	stay
today	upstairs	drink	sure	busy
such	follow	from	because	cannot
without	start	jump	beginning	something
tonight	football	away	plenty	quickly
think	noise	paper	finish	hurry
teacher	feel	under	silly	afraid
teacher	few	black	forest	birthday
door	please	white	below	touch
children	even	chair	write	music
another	clever	smell	afraid	scream
smile	neat	throw	buy	weather
while	heard	slow	move	rainbow
wait	door	fast	use	please
body	child	old	blood	many
place	blame	wake	break	better
thank	air	close	steal	feel
cost	slow	open	should	world
lift	garden	blow	none	forget
itself	forget	join	hungry	town
seem	start	sound	sometimes	paper
find	own	grow	return	sugar
sleep	dream	easy	bottom	dark
suppose	happily	ever	after	huge
quick	inside	street	sudden	young
bedroom	outside	happen	weak	class

pain	care	fight	strong	ready
two	afraid	loud	beautiful	danger
one	down	down	grown	awful
few	return	turn	hurt	use
close	surprise	finish	soft	spring
scream	stuck	drop	stop	family
city	lady	notice	manage	someone
myself	night	outside	inside	village
splash	hope	burn	smoke	flew
throw	town	draw	blow	grew

Now that you have finished Book 1, well done!!

Now go straight on to the next level -

Spelling & Word-Power Skills - Book 2

Answers page 35 Ggap-filling			Answers page 37 Opposites			Answers page 37/38 Gap-filling	
1	train		sad	*happy*		read	
2	plate		public	*secret*		secret	
3	Tail		serious	*funny*		money	
4	date		part	*complete*		turkey	
5	mistake		shallow	*deep*		deep	
6	skate		learn	*teach*		feed	
7	wait		hungry	*feed*		taxi	
8	holiday		mountain	*valley*		reason	
9	bake		receive	*give*		meat	
10	pane		generous	*mean*		teeth	
11	paid					tree	
12	gate					heat	
13	mane					peaches	
14	sage					wheels	
15	paid					bleach	

Answers page 40 - *Long I*			Answers page 40 - *Opposites*	
tight	slide		day	*night*
fright	delight		loose	*tight*
reply	might		narrow	*wide*
knight	wine		seek	*hide*
supplier	right		laugh	*cry*
night	spied		dark	*bright*
tonight	fried		low	*high*
magnify	thigh		truth	*lie*
drive	cried		left	*right*
			born	*die*

Answers page 40/41 *Gap-filling*	Answers page 42 Complete Word - *Long o*		Answers page 43 *Opposites*	
drives	drove	woke	young	*old*
tried	hope	grow	sink	*float*
hide	throat	toe	friend	*foe*
fried	coat	gold	lead	*follow*
right	moat		let go	*hold*
thigh	throw		buck	*doe*
bright	float		yes	*no*
tonight	boat		hide	*show*
pie	slope		**Answers page 43 – *Gap Filling***		
magnify	blow		goat	note	snow
cry	roast		blow	throw	
reply	stone		follow	float	
tight	follow		coat	snow	
height	gateau		elbow	hole	
delight	elbow		woke	although	
	old		own	goat	

Answers page 45 Long U	Answers page 46 Oo words	Answers page 49 Gap-filling – oi & oy	Answers page 51 St & Sl - Gap-filling
Roots	book	boil	slow/slug
Should	look	toy	slam
Stood	pool	boy	nest
Route	broom	noise	stamp
Tooth	tooth	coin	sleep
Spoon	food	enjoy	must
Through	soon	spoil	slide
Refuse	moon	voice	just
True	mood	moist	west
Coupon	hood	ointment	past
Nephew	good		slurp
Soup	hook		twist
New	noon		fist
Glue	roof		star
Chew			slim
			Front
			Slot
			Nest
			sleet

Answers page 52 Gap –filling - sh	Answers page 53/54 Gap-filling - sp	Answers page 55/56 Gap-filling - dr & cr	Answers page 57 br & cr - Opposites	Answers page 58 Gap-filling br/cr
Sheep	spider	drink	*sister*	bruise
Shop	spend	crowd	*bride*	gravy
Wash	special	crown	*grand*	briefcase
Shape	sports	crisp	*brilliant*	brisk
Sharp	spill	dress	*brave*	grandchild
Should	speak	creepy	*broken/break*	breeze
Show	spread	drag	*grief*	brake
Fish	spell	drill	*bright*	growl
Shelf	wasp	drenched		grief
	Hospital	cream		brigade
	Spare	crowd		gracefully
	Speed	crack		breathe
	Spuds	drum		grasped
	Spears	dribbles		governor
	Spy	driveway		break
	Suspect			
	Sponge			
	Clasped			
	Spit			
	suspense			

Answers page 59/60 Gap-filling - ai			Answers page 61/62 Gap-filling – i_e		
Main	paint	frail	hide	fire	wipe limes
Afraid	praise		mine	like	nine
Paid	bait		shine	fire	grime
Fail	pain		live	bike	bite
Wait	sail		vine	slide	time
Refrain	grain		hive	tile	beside
Pail	tail		bike	wine	pride

© 2018 Roselle Thompson

Spelling &Word-Power Skills Book 1

Certificate of Achievement

This **Phoenix Certificate** is presented to

....

For successfully completing

Spelling & Word-Power Skills Book 1

Score Achieved ☐

Comment..

....

Teacher/Parent Signature..

Date..

About the Author

Roselle Thompson B.A Hons, MPhil, FRSA, has over 27 years of experience in teaching and education development in the UK, from nursery to University levels. In addition to her academic lecturing and writing, Roselle has been creating, since 1994, intensive courses in a number of subjects; including English (language and literature), Verbal Reasoning and Public Speaking for children from as young as 5 years old, to GCSE Secondary and A level 6th Form. Roselle also organises extra support Tutorials for Undergraduates struggling in their first year at university. As a Broadcaster, Poet and International Speaker; her approach is therefore to make her significantly accumulated skills available to her students for their personal empowerment, development and life-long success.

BOOKS IN THE SERIES, BY THE SAME AUTHOR...............

ENGLISH GRAMMAR: A STUDENT'S COMPANION

This book prepares children for the 11+ independent and state grammar schools as well as the Key Stage 2 SATs tests and Common Entrance at 13 years. Although there are a variety of grammar books on the market, this book is based on over 27 years of the Author's techniques based on teaching and heading schools and rigorously tested exercises done in both school and tuition classrooms. The book contains a thorough preparation in grammar, and has valuable exercises for all aspects of foundation English literacy development to Secondary level education and beyond.

MASTERING COMPREHENSION SKILLS

This book provides a complete package of introduction, revision and practice comprehension passages to help you with preparation for the Key Stage 2 SATs tests and those preparing for the 11+ independent and state grammar school tests at 13. The format of the questions replicates the SATs Reading and Comprehension tests to help your child become familiar with the format of the tests.

VOCABULARY SKILLS FOR STUDENTS & TEACHERS

The Vocabulary book contains over 60 Units and 60 Unit Tests which can be used as lessons, with a total of 600 vocabulary words. Each Unit presents at least 10 vocabulary words which show their class or part of speech, together with their definition. This is followed by 60 gap-filling worksheet exercises for you to complete, without looking at the meaning. Each gap-filling exercise helps students to see how these words are used in their contexts and tests the child's knowledge of them. Check out the 39 general knowledge challenges set throughout the book as well as 16 interesting brain-teasing crossword puzzles!

SPELLING & WORD POWER SKILLS

This structured spelling course was written to develop essential spelling skills for both individual use and group work in the classroom. It will help you to learn spelling techniques to improve your vocabulary knowledge and develop your word-power skills. It is designed to encourage you to read and understand how words are formed, their relationship with each other, followed by practical spelling activities.

The books in the **Spelling & Word-Power Series** cover 3 levels of practice, arranged from **Starters** (which introduces the structure of words, sounds and rules), **Level 1** (expands knowledge of phonics and increases the level of structuring of words and rules which guide them), **Level 2** and **Level 3** (provides more challenges in exercises and rules that provides a structure within which the child is equipped with more advanced tools to learn, understand and spell at more advanced levels). Each level introduces spelling concepts, with explanation to help establish the rules which guide the approach to spelling techniques at each grade. Rules are identified and practice is given in exercises that test understanding. Practice exercises for you to complete, test your understanding of the rules applied. In this book, to help you spell correctly, there are spelling strategies that look at the certain aspects of the sound, structure and spelling of words. Additionally, some word-hunt challenges help you to become aware of the origin of words, forcing a closer look at the rules and word formation.

Teachers will find this book useful as the exercises here can either be used in group work or for individual learners to use at their own pace in the classroom and for extended work at home. This book therefore has a dual purpose – it not only teaches and expands but tests students' overall mastery of their spelling as they develop. Also included in the book is your reward, a **Certificate of Achievement**, which marks your successful completion of this book.

CPSIA information can be obtained
at www.ICGtesting.com
Printed in the USA
LVHW060435221021
701182LV00014B/93